Bolsover Castle

Paul Drury

La gallerie

Croupades sur les voltes à main gauche

CONTENTS

Facing page: These putti on the Venus Fountain, playful symbols of masculine potency, are modern recreations, based on surviving fragments

Left: Aerial view of Bolsover Castle from the west. The Little Castle stands on the end of a promontory with the terrace along the top of the escarpment

Below left: A plan showing the main features of the medieval castle superimposed (in red) on the existing landscape. The medieval great tower was probably much smaller than the 17th-century Little Castle. Burials in the inner bailey were probably associated with a castle chapel; those in the outer bailey may relate to a churchyard displaced by the castle (see page 33)

Tour

THE MEDIEVAL CASTLE

Bolsover Castle occupies a superb vantage point, towering over the vale below. The 17th-century castle here today was built on top of the earthworks and ruins of the medieval castle.

The outer gate, by the visitor centre, has remained in its original, 12th-century position. It leads into the outer bailey, or castle yard, whose medieval defences are visible on the north-east side, with an 18th-century wall on top of the eroded bank. The Riding House Range, on the far side of the outer bailey, stands more or less over the defences of the inner bailey, the predecessor of the great court.

Beyond the inner bailey was the medieval inner court, surrounded by a massive polygonal stone wall. It was lowered and remodelled as the garden wall that now skirts the Little Castle, the first of the 17th-century structures at Bolsover, built by Charles Cavendish between 1612 and 1617. In 1200 a deer park was enclosed at the foot of the castle walls, extending westwards down to the river Doe Lea. This provided a foreground of wood and pasture to the panoramic views to the north and west, and still influenced the character of the landscape in the 17th century.

The Terrace Range, forming the west side of the great court, was the second of the Cavendish buildings. It was completed by 1634 but was partly rebuilt in the 1660s. The Riding House Range was the third and final Cavendish building at Bolsover.

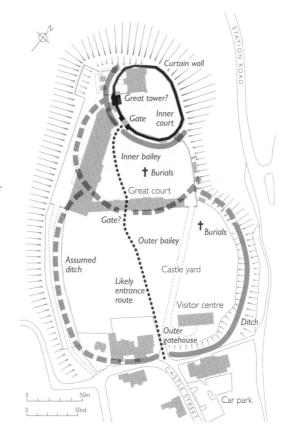

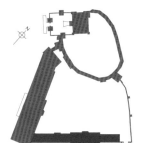

Ground floor

Right: The Riding House Range seen from across the great court. From the left: the shoeing house and smithy, the riding house and the stable

Below: Design for a doorcase by Alessandro Francini, from his Livre d'Architecture (Paris 1631), which inspired the design of those of the Riding House Range

Below right: A portrait by Sir Anthony van Dyck of Charles I on horseback, 1633, accompanied by the Chevalier de St Antoine, who taught William Cavendish the art of manège

RIDING HOUSE RANGE

William Cavendish was a keen horseman and an expert in the art of *manège*, which was a form of dressage. The Riding House Range was devoted to housing, training and maintaining his horses. It was built in about 1660, essentially in one operation from west to east, and consists of three sections: on the left, a smithy and shoeing house with a viewing gallery above; in the middle, a riding house; and on the right, a stable, all with lodgings in the garrets.

1 Stable and **2** Lodgings

Manège horses were highly valued, and their status is reflected in the sophisticated architectural detailing of the stable. It has a grand doorcase, flanked by pairs of tall mullioned windows. Inside, there was a plaster cornice, still visible at the east end. About 15 horses could be stalled along the back wall, which originally had no windows (see drawing on pages 10–11). In the stable at Welbeck Abbey, Cavendish's main house, horses were stalled facing the gangway for much of the day.

The stable was subsequently converted into a pair of two-room apartments, probably under the 2nd Duke of Newcastle in the late 1680s. Windows were cut into the south wall and fireplaces were constructed in the end walls to heat the principal rooms, and in the corners of the inner rooms. The horses were moved to the former long gallery in the Terrace Range.

All but the east end of this block was unroofed by 1827. The roof was largely rebuilt by the Ministry of Works in the 20th century and covers not only the stable but also, at its west end, defined by the scars of a cross wall, a former stairwell with a lodging behind the surviving wall. The garret over the stable was not the usual hayloft but a space with fireplaces at either end, intended to accommodate stable staff or lesser-ranking visitors during major entertainments. Hay was probably stored in a now-lost barn in the outer court, which by the 18th century was divided into paddocks. Grooms could reach the paddocks directly via the doorway under the stair.

Le galop a Gauche.

Le vray galop a Droicte.

Au pas a Gauche.

Meusg. le Marquis.

Au pas a Droicte.

Trot a Gauche.

Trot a Droicte.

Left: William Cavendish (centre) giving Captain Mazin a riding lesson, from his book La Méthode nouvelle et invention extraordinaire de dresser les chevaux *(1658), engraved by Lucas Vorstermans II, after Abraham van Diepenbeke*

Below: William Cavendish's leather saddle, which he used to ride manège *horses, c.1650s. William was one of the best riders in Europe. His training methods, based on mutual respect between horse and rider rather than brute force, are still followed*

The Art and Status of *Manège*

William Cavendish was a keen horseman, writing a seminal book about riding in 1658.

Manège, or *haute école*, is the art of training or 'dressing' horses to execute set movements on spoken command. The horse is trained to carry more weight on the hind than the forequarters as it moves, rearing and leaping in a relatively confined space. Originating in Renaissance Italy in about 1500, the art was rapidly assimilated into European courtly culture, reaching England through a Spanish gift of horses to Henry VIII in 1514.

As a boy of ten, William Cavendish was sent to learn the art from the Chevalier de St Antoine, who arrived in England in 1603 with a coronation gift of six *manège* horses from the French king to James I. James preferred hunting but his elder son, Prince Henry, took to *manège* with enthusiasm, with William as one of his riding companions. The patronage of the young prince's Court, carried on after his death in 1612 by his brother, Charles (the future Charles I), ensured the high status of *manège* in England until the Civil War. Riding houses were built by many noblemen, following

Prince Henry's example. They were a predominantly English development from open-air *manège* yards, in response to the colder English climate.

After the Restoration in 1660, Charles II's Court was more interested in racing horses than riding them. While William Cavendish's devotion continued unabated, *manège* was less popular among the English aristocracy. He seems to have anticipated the shift in his book *La Méthode nouvelle et invention extraordinaire de dresser les chevaux*, published in 1658 and translated in 1743: 'I presume those great wits (the sneering gentlemen) will give Kings, Princes, and persons of quality leave to love pleasure-horses, as being an exercise that is very noble, and that which makes them appear most graceful when they shew themselves to their subjects, or at the head of an army, to animate it, so that the easure in this case is as useful as anything else, besides the glory and satisfaction that attends it.'

5

Ground floor

Right: The Riding House Range from the castle yard. The four large windows on the left were inserted in the stable in the late 17th century, when it was converted into apartments

Below: One of William Cavendish's manège horses, shown before the east front of Welbeck Abbey, his main seat, c.1630

When the adjacent state apartment was rebuilt about 1666, the upper lodging room beyond the stair was upgraded with the addition of two closets, mirroring those provided for the state bedchamber directly underneath. It is likely to have been used by William Cavendish's Master of the Horse, Captain Mazin, with the smaller room below (now the visitor toilets) as his business or tack room. He had similar accommodation at Cavendish's other riding house and stable at Welbeck.

3 Riding House, 4 Shoeing House and 5 Smithy

The riding house is the focus of the range, both in its height and its function. Entered through a grand

doorway, similar to but larger than that of the stable, it is well lit by large mullioned windows in both long walls. These were at first set lower but were then raised, most probably before the building was roofed, so that the horses would not be distracted by what was going on outside. The restored floor is made of sand, on which horses were schooled around a pillar.

The elaborate roof dates mainly from about 1660 and was not intended to be seen. When it was repaired in the late 19th century, the original garret floor and flat plaster ceilings between the tie beams were removed, presumably to make the space appear more archaic. The decorative pendants were probably added at the same time. Inspired by a drawing by the architect John Smythson (see page 35) for Cavendish's 1623 riding house at Welbeck, they were perhaps even removed from there.

High in the east wall is a window from the viewing gallery, originally fitted with opening timber casements on the inside. The window consists of a central arched opening flanked by smaller flat-headed lights and is known as a *serliana* or Venetian window. In the 17th century, this form of window was particularly associated with sovereignty. Here it was used by guests, friends and ultimately by an ageing William Cavendish, viewing his horses being schooled below. The off-centre axis of the riding house doorways – and hence the placing of the window – was dictated by the functional layout of the stable. The doorway below the viewing gallery leads to the shoeing house, lit only by a pair of external doors (one of which is now blocked), which would have been open when the farrier was at work. Beyond is the smithy (now the Education Room), which retains a hood over the hearth.

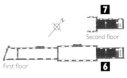

Left: Interior of the riding house, looking east to the viewing gallery. There were originally flat plaster ceilings between the tie beams, lost in the 19th century, which would have made it appear more like a great hall and less like a barn

Below: Portrait of Margaret Cavendish, William's wife (see page 43), by Peter van Lisebetten, after Abraham van Diepenbeke

'[The horses] seemed to rejoice whensoever he came into the Stables, by their trampling action, and the noise they made; nay they would go much better in the Mannage, when my Lord was by.'
Margaret Cavendish, writing about her husband, William, in 1667

6 Viewing Gallery and 7 Lodging

An elegant shallow stair at the east end of the range led to a well-appointed first-floor apartment. Its fireplaces were set within panelling to the height of the doors. The inner room, containing the viewing window, has a decorative plaster frieze derived from designs published in 1565 by a Flemish architect, Hans Vredeman de Vries. Such

an old-fashioned design does not necessarily mean that this room pre-dates the Civil War; it is perfectly possible that this style continued to appeal to William Cavendish. The lodging rooms on the top floor were connected through the garrets over the riding house and stable to the western stair. The glazed doorway now provides a fine vantage point from which to admire the roof structure.

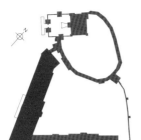

Ground floor

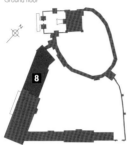

Basement

Right: The Terrace Range
seen from the great court,
as modified in the 1660s,
with the hall behind the four
tall windows

TERRACE RANGE

William Cavendish developed the Terrace Range in stages between the late 1620s and the 1660s. At first, it was almost symmetrical on the side facing the terrace – a house two rooms deep with a hall facing the courtyard. But once it had reached first-floor level, in about 1630, the architect John Smythson supplied a plan to extend it southwards (see page 38), with a long gallery, backed by a state apartment. This change in plan transformed a conventional house into a huge, extravagant pavilion for reception and entertainment. The shell was probably completed before Cavendish entertained Charles I and Henrietta Maria at Bolsover in 1634 (see page 39), although in place of the intended chapel at the south end, a smaller one was contrived on the top floor at the north end.

In about 1650, during the Commonwealth, the gallery, state apartment and probably the hall were plundered for their building materials, particularly for the lead and timber of their flat roofs. William re-roofed the hall in about 1660, but instead of replacing the flat roof, he covered it with a steep cross-gabled roof containing garrets. These were lit by windows in the pedimented scrolled gables

facing the great court. The earlier straight gables to the north, between the hall and the chapel, were altered to match, regularizing the roof line. The architectural details are similar in many respects to those in the Riding House Range. Then, with his architect Samuel Marsh, Cavendish rebuilt the state apartment behind the gallery between 1663 and 1666. The coat of arms above the door bears his arms as Duke of Newcastle, to which rank he was elevated in March 1665.

The impractical magnificence of the remodelled Terrace Range was short lived. The state apartment was probably dismantled by William's son Henry in the late 1680s. The gallery then became a stable, with a brewhouse at its north end. By the early 1770s, the whole range was a roofless ruin.

8 Basement

The basement with its high-level windows dates from the late 1620s. Because it was little altered after 1634, it gives a unique insight into the organization of service rooms of the time and the scale and sophistication considered necessary to support royal entertainment. The kitchens are not connected to the beer and wine cellars

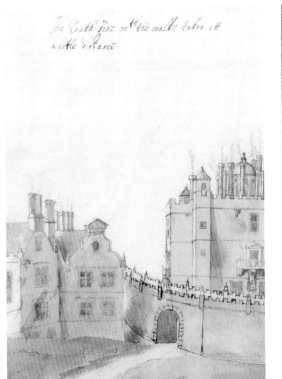

View into the basement and service rooms

A Remains of charcoal stoves in the inner kitchen, back to back with the remains of those in the outer kitchen

B The roasting hearth in the outer kitchen, flanked by warm cupboards

C Serving hatch

D Arcade which carried a wall forming a withdrawing chamber at the end of the 1630s gallery

E Door cut in the end of the gallery when the wall above the arcade was removed in the 1660s; it was blocked in the 1680s when this area became the brewhouse

F Sockets for beams carrying a floor inserted in the brewhouse conversion

at the north end at this level, reflecting the division in household organization between the clerk of the kitchen and the butler. Each was served by separate stairs both from the great court and up to the principal floor (see plans on inside back cover).

There is an inner and outer kitchen, each originally with a roasting hearth and a bank of charcoal stoves for preparing more delicate dishes. The outer kitchen also had stone cupboards flanking, and so kept warm by, the roasting hearth. The arcade was inserted in about 1630 to support the change of plan in the rooms on the floor above. On the east side is the pastry with its bank of ovens. The boiling house originally had one, and possibly two, metal vats, used for simmering food, set in masonry with fires beneath, within the fireplace opening. All these rooms are close to the serving place (which originally also had a direct connection to the terrace), where food was assembled and dressed before being taken upstairs. Beyond, off the corridor, are the larders: the wet larder, with drain channels in the floor, for raw meat and fish; probably the dairy larder adjacent, for processing milk and storing butter and cheese, with a small fireplace, since it could

not function if too cold; and the dry larder for dry stores and cooked foods. Off the inner kitchen was the clerk of the kitchen's room, once vaulted with a small fireplace and a hatch through to the plate scullery, a vaulted room where silver and silver-gilt plate could be securely stored and cleaned after use. The adjacent stair provided service access to the great court. The remains of a brick firebox for a brewing vat, built into the corner of the inner kitchen, belong to the late 17th century, when the kitchens became the lower level of a brewhouse for making beer.

Top left: Drawing of the Terrace Range in the 1630s showing the hall (left) with a crenellated parapet around a flat roof and the adjacent rooms to the right with straight gables

Below: John Smythson's design for a roasting hearth for the outer kitchen with a vertical coal fire held behind iron bars; it was also fitted with a chimney crane

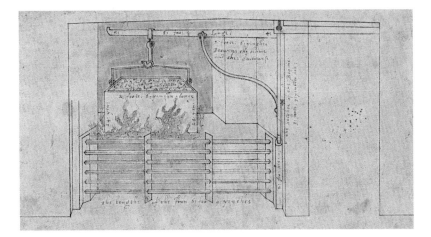

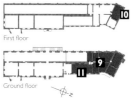

First floor

Ground floor

The hall looking north, with the kitchen service rooms below and garrets above

A The pastry

B The boiling house

C The doors from the entry and the service area

D The buffet recess, and the fireplace replaced in about 1660

E Fireplace in the garret added in about 1660

Cutaway reconstruction drawing of the Terrace and Riding House Ranges from the south, in about 1670

A Dry larder

B Boiling house

C Pastry

D Dining room

E Withdrawing room

F Lodging room

G Flat roof with balcony overlooking the vale

H Stable with accommodation over

I Paddock in castle yard

J Great court

9 Northern Rooms and 10 Chapel

The ground-floor and first-floor rooms of the northern end of the Terrace Range are best seen from the basement. The lobby at ground-floor level above the basement serving place marks the centre of the late 1620s building and led into a passage behind the screen at the low end of the hall (see plans on inside back cover). This was also the point at which service routes from the kitchens and cellars converged, with the pantry (for the service of bread) and the buttery (for the service of drink) at the head of the cellar stair beyond. The north end of the range, completed to the original plan, contained mostly small lodging chambers arranged around the main stair, with a two-room apartment at the north end at ground-floor level. The pair of rooms above, also reached from the garden wall-walk, formed the chapel with an inner chamber; their fireplaces were added only after 1660.

The break in construction around first-floor level is clearly visible from the basement. It marks the abrupt change of intention in about 1630, when Smythson redesigned and greatly extended the southern end of the range. The use of flat stone and occasionally brick arches, rather than timber lintels over openings, and the extraordinary number of cupboards built into the walls are unusual details, characteristic of all the Cavendish buildings at Bolsover before 1660.

11 Hall

The hall was traditionally where the household ate together. By the time it was built, however, William Cavendish, his close family and guests would normally have eaten in a great chamber beyond, while the servants dined in the hall, presided over by the steward on a dais at the south end. Only on exceptional occasions would

Cavendish have eaten in the hall, when the buffet recess in the west wall next to the fireplace would have been conspicuously decked with plate. But it remained the normal room of entry from the terrace via the screens passage, and the route to the state apartment. Under its shallow-pitch leaded roof, it was open through two storeys, looking rather like the riding house before its ceiling was removed.

When the flat roof of the hall was replaced with a new cross-gabled roof in about 1660, the stair at the south end was adapted to provide access to the new garrets and the flat roof of the gallery. The hall now had a flat corniced ceiling, and a new fireplace in the same style as the riding house doorways. The walls remained plastered above panelling up to the tall window cills.

Ground floor

Right: Portrait of King Charles II
as a boy, in armour, in about
1638, by the studio of Sir
Anthony van Dyck, which
once hung in the withdrawing
room at Bolsover
Below: The monumental
entrance to the state
apartment from the great
court, with the arms of William
Cavendish as Duke of
Newcastle over the doorcase

12 State Apartment

John Smythson designed the first state apartment in
the Terrace Range for William Cavendish in the
early 1630s (see plan, page 38). It was where
Cavendish would have entertained his most
important guests. It was probably complete, though
possibly not fully fitted out, by the time Charles I
and Henrietta Maria came to Bolsover in 1634. In
about 1650, during the Commonwealth, however, it
was severely damaged, and it was rebuilt between
1663 and 1667 in an Italian Mannerist style.

At this time, the layout was simplified to three
substantial rooms: a dining room, a withdrawing
room and a lodging room. The doors between the
rooms were also realigned, so that there was a
clear view through from room to room and a
sense of progress through the apartment. The
spine wall was cut back to maximize the width of
the rooms, so all the visible masonry dates from
the mid 1660s, apart from the north wall of the
dining room, where all the building phases of the
Terrace Range can be seen.

But, more dramatically, the state apartment was
now entered directly from the great court, rather
than through the hall. The stair which led up to the
entry to the hall from the terrace was removed (if
it had not already been dismantled under the
Commonwealth), so the hall was left firmly within
the service end of the building and thus functioned
as a servants' hall. This reflects the decline in status
of the hall, which was no longer a place where the
whole household dined together; it also fixes its
date to between 1660 and 1665, when society was
re-established after the Restoration of Charles II.

Interiors of the State Apartment

The walls of the new state rooms were panelled,
with cornices beneath deeply coved ceilings (see
pages 10–11). Plaster cross-vaults admitted light
from an upper tier of windows, inspired by vaulted
rooms in Italian palaces. The stone doorcases and
window reveals were left exposed, although they
were probably painted. The iron fixings, still visible
in the window reveals, suggest that the lower, large
window lights had French casements, which
opened into the room; they were very rarely used
in England other than occasionally for doors, as in
the Little Castle. This choice probably reflects
Cavendish's familiarity with continental taste after
his exile in Paris and Antwerp during the Civil War.

Ground floor

13 Dining Room

A monumental rusticated Corinthian doorcase, the architectural focus of the great court, leads into the dining room. Above the door are the arms of Cavendish as Duke of Newcastle. Directly opposite, another elaborate doorcase frames the view through the spine wall and gallery to the countryside beyond, called in the building accounts the 'Bellavista'. The plain face of the other side of this doorway, on the gallery side, emphasizes that the principal entry into this new building was from the great court, with an exit via the gallery to the terrace.

14 Withdrawing Room and 15 Lodging Room

The withdrawing room was a place to retire to after dinner and also probably for entertainment. The lodging room contained a state bed set on the east wall, behind a balustrade. Traces of a plaster cornice survive, marking the springing of the lost coved ceiling. Bassano recorded a sequence of dynastic portraits in these rooms in the 1680s, emphasizing William's noble lineage and the family's connections to the restored monarchy. The low door from the lodging room led to a dressing room and 'Stoolehouse', containing a close stool and pan (chamber pot). These were built as an afterthought in the gap between this block and the Riding House Range.

Hangings, furnishings and pictures would have provided colour and richness in the state apartment. Richard Bassano, deputy herald for Staffordshire and Derbyshire, who visited Bolsover in the 1680s, wrote that all the chimney pieces were of 'Blew and white marble', 'blew' being the near-black polished Derbyshire limestone.

Left: William Cavendish by the studio of Sir Anthony van Dyck. His sash was originally red, for the Order of the Bath, but it was later overpainted when he was invested as a knight of the Garter in 1661. The original Van Dyck portrait, on which this version is based, hung in the withdrawing room at Bolsover
Below: Banquet at Night, by Wolfgang Heimbach, 1640. Although set in northern Europe, it gives a good idea of how a large dining room would have been used

Ground floor

Right: The long gallery at Hardwick Hall, Derbyshire, probably designed by Robert Smythson, is hung with tapestries and portraits, as the gallery at Bolsover would have been

Below: The Bolsover gallery, as remodelled in the 1660s, seen through the large doorway inserted in the south wall in the late 17th century (the low blocking wall is modern)

16 Gallery

Long galleries were typically used for exercise and recreation, but this one was probably envisaged primarily as a place for entertaining large numbers of people. In the early 1630s, there were withdrawing chambers at either end, probably intended to display smaller works of art. The scars of their walls are visible, together with the arcade inserted across the outer kitchen to carry the northern one. The gallery was originally panelled up to a plaster cornice below a deep plaster frieze, possibly with decorative painting. When the gallery was re-roofed in the 1660s, the withdrawing chambers were eliminated, the chimney pieces were moved and a direct connection to the service rooms was made at the north end. The walls were probably then fully panelled, but no detail survives. Bassano recorded only one notable picture here in the 1680s: 'And here in a large Frame is placed ye Picture of Wm Duke/ of New Castle in Armour on Horseback w[i]th a Trunchon/ in 's hand/ Below are Men and Horses in Severall postures/ as of an army defeated; & under Written/ LA BATAILLE GAIGNE[E].'

In 1674, William began a new ducal palace at Nottingham Castle, completed after his death by his son Henry. Its state apartment seems to have supplanted the one at Bolsover, which was dismantled, having lost any practical function. A casual documentary reference suggests this began in 1687. The basement wall was then extended upwards, and the north end of the gallery, with the basement below, became a brewhouse. An additional floor was inserted, corresponding with the transom level of the windows. The conversion of the southern end of the gallery to a stable was facilitated by cutting the large round-headed doorway through the south wall. It was connected by a roughly cut doorway to the former lodging room, which was probably used as a hay store.

17 Terrace

The terrace was originally the drive to the front door of the Little Castle, begun in 1612, and later also served as the approach to the Terrace Range. It was formed by reconfiguring the earthworks of the western side of the medieval castle. After the mid 1660s, once the principal entrance to the Terrace Range moved to the great court, it

became primarily a garden terrace, with a viewing platform at the north end.

This side of the Terrace Range is more unified than the great court elevation, but it became so comparatively late. The doorway towards the northern end, now without its stair, marks the centre of William Cavendish's first building, its northern block built at an angle along the line of the inner court ditch. We know from a 1630s drawing that originally each bay was straight gabled. John Smythson grafted a new gallery onto this half-built house, to a highly inventive design. The shafts between the windows were perhaps inspired by the cannon columns in the frontispiece to *The Gunner* (1628), emphasizing the martial character of the castle, but Smythson added voluts at the top, derived from the capitals of Ionic columns, hinting at an Italian villa on a hill. The geometric-shaped gables on the northern block were added as the building was being finished, in about 1633. They give architectural emphasis to the top floor and probably relate to William's decision to use it as the chapel – the lantern finials suggesting Christ as the light of the world. Architectural coherence was finally achieved in the 1660s, when the remaining gables on this side were concealed behind a parapet and shafts were inserted into the elevation below, matching those on the gallery.

From the terrace there is a panoramic view of the Doe Lea valley below the limestone scarp, as far as the edge of the Peak District. The medieval park once covered the land down to the stream. In the 17th century this was a rich agricultural landscape, containing two other contemporary tall houses: Owlcotes, built by William's grandmother, Bess of Hardwick, and now lost; and Sutton (Scarsdale) Hall, built by Francis Leke. It was a powerful landscape in every sense, its houses built with the proceeds of coal pits beneath it. The view was reshaped first by industrial mining from the late 19th century, and then by the closure of the pits in the late 20th century. The principal legacy of the mining industry is New Bolsover, laid out in 1893 by the Bolsover Colliery Company as a model garden village.

Above: Bolsover Castle from the west in the 1630s; from this viewpoint down the slope, the basement of the Terrace Range is obscured. The door to the left marks the centre of the Terrace Range as first conceived in the 1620s. It also shows the pre-1660s form of the gateway to the Little Castle forecourt

Left: The gallery elevation to the terrace; the stair dates from the 1660s restoration and originally had balustrades

Below: Frontispiece from Robert Norton, The Gunner *(1628). Smythson was perhaps influenced by the unusual design of the columns*

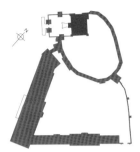

THE LITTLE CASTLE

'Sir Charles [Cavendish] had buylt a delicate little house', according to an anonymous writer in 1618. The Little Castle he built between 1612 and 1617 is indeed an exquisite miniature house or lodge. Tall and self-contained, it was a place to which the Cavendish family could retire from the formality of life at their main residence at Welbeck. Although entirely new, it resembled a Norman great tower domesticated and modernized over a long time, suggesting the ancient lineage of its owners.

The formal approach to the Little Castle is from the terrace, through a forecourt with false arrow loops, heightening the sense of antiquity. The steps, which are missing their balustrades, and

Below: The Little Castle from the south-east. The scarcity of windows on this elevation emphasizes its resemblance to a Norman great tower

the gateway date from after the dismantling of the strong walls of the castle by Parliamentarian forces in the Civil War.

There are four lodges in the forecourt. Their interiors were well appointed, with Smythson fireplaces like the garden rooms (see page 30), suggesting quite high-status use, perhaps as lodgings, except for the one on the south, which was probably the first bathhouse.

Visitors enter the Little Castle through a porch with a Gothic fan vault in the middle of a classical, symmetrical façade. Above, Hercules holds up the balcony on his back, just as in classical mythology, in the eleventh of his twelve labours, he held up the world for Atlas, while Atlas retrieved the apples of the Hesperides. The balcony and doorcase above the entrance were installed by Charles Cavendish's son William, who finished the interiors of the house by 1621.

The Little Castle is extremely clever in its use of space. There is a clear, although circuitous, route through the house, from being received at the front door to progressing, according to one's rank and standing, perhaps even as far as Cavendish's bedchamber on the first floor. The circuitous planning is reminiscent of Charles's mother's house, Hardwick Hall.

18 Anteroom

The use of this small room is a puzzle. It is very unusual in 17th-century England to have a richly decorated, heated room next to the entrance to a house. It could have been used for welcoming visitors, but its position to one side of the route to the main stair, combined with its obvious status, suggests that visitors having business with William would have been received and entertained here.

The paintings in the lunettes are allegories of three of the four classical temperaments: melancholic (introverted and thoughtful – the old man and girl, above the door); choleric (ambitious and passionate – the soldier and his mistress); and phlegmatic (relaxed and stable – the fisherman and fishwife). They were copied from engravings by Pieter de Jode from designs by Maarten de Vos (1532–1603), a Flemish artist who provided the source material for much decorative art in England at the time. The absence of the fourth temperament – sanguine (high-spirited and sociable) – is a mystery, but perhaps William

Ground floor

Far left: The anteroom looking east, with the allegory of the melancholic temperament over the door

Left and above: The allegory of the choleric temperament from the anteroom (top) and the source engraving (below) by Pieter de Jode after Maarten de Vos, c.1600

Below left: The hall, which was used as a dining and reception space

Cavendish himself completed the sequence, as he stood under the four Elements – earth, air, fire and water – on the far wall.

By about 1670 this room was called 'the little roome next the hall stares', and was furnished with a table and eight chairs. The closet, a feature common to all the corner rooms in the castle, contained a close stool and pan (chamber pot). The entrance lobby to the hall has a door, high up in the wall, to a vaulted chamber which was probably the porter's lodging, reached by a ladder.

19 Hall

The hall was used as a dining space for the household and as a reception space for guests. The architecture is a curious hybrid of classical Doric columns and Gothic pointed rib vaults, perhaps to suggest a modernized medieval stone hall. It was originally finished with lined false ashlar joints to resemble stone. The layout is similar to that of a medieval hall, with the raised stool closet floor suggesting a dais on the east and the position of the doors implying a service passage on the west. The chimney piece is dated 1616; to its left is

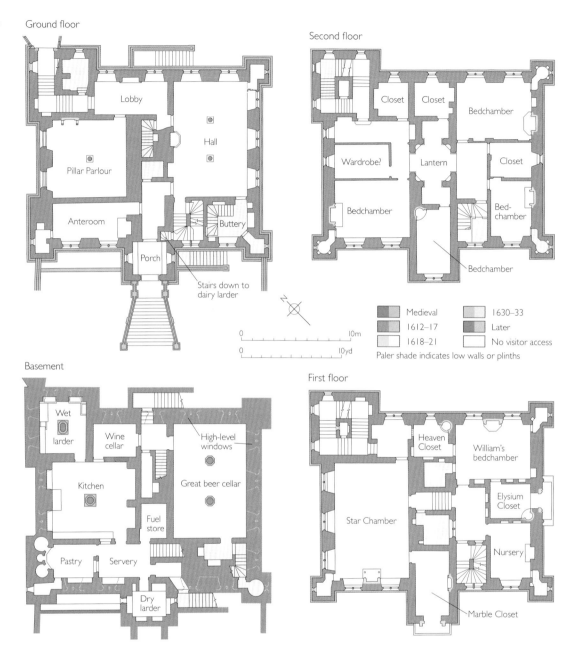

Right: Floor plans of the Little Castle. The porter's lodging (off the entrance lobby) and the probable dairy larder (the cheese room) under the porch, both on mezzanine levels, are not shown

Ground floor

Lobby

Hall

Pillar Parlour

Anteroom

Buttery

Porch

Stairs down to dairy larder

Second floor

Closet

Closet

Bedchamber

Wardrobe?

Lantern

Closet

Bedchamber

Bed-chamber

Bedchamber

Medieval

1612–17

1618–21

1630–33

Later

No visitor access

Paler shade indicates low walls or plinths

Basement

Wet larder

Wine cellar

High-level windows

Kitchen

Great beer cellar

Fuel store

Pastry

Servery

Dry larder

First floor

Heaven Closet

William's bedchamber

Star Chamber

Elysium Closet

Nursery

Marble Closet

a buffet recess, reminiscent of the one in the hall in the Terrace Range.

The hall was planned by Charles and adapted by William, who was probably responsible for the level floor, inserting the panelling and commissioning the paintings in the lunettes. These continue the theme of Hercules seen on the balcony. The figures were copied from engravings by Antonio Tempesta, published in 1608, but they are set against painted extensions of the hall vaulting, to create the illusion that the figures are actually in the room. The story of Hercules was a popular allegory

of human nature – he had the potential for evil, since he killed his children in a fit of madness, but also the power to do good, since he atoned through his great labours. In the lunettes, Hercules is shown performing four of his twelve labours: slaying the Nemean lion; capturing the boar of Erymanthus; capturing the Cretan bull; and stealing the mares of Diomedes. To the sides of the chimney piece he is shown with Vulcan, god of Fire. From the high end of the hall, the door leads past the stair from the wine cellar to a large heated lobby at the foot of the great stair.

20 Pillar Parlour

William Cavendish and his guests used the Pillar Parlour as a dining room. The elaborate panelling is based on that in the great chamber of Theobalds Palace, Hertfordshire, drawn by John Smythson in 1618. The original black and gold paint scheme survives on a panel next to the chimney piece; the rest is a modern restoration. The paintings depict the five senses and are adapted from engravings by Cornelius Cort after Frans Floris. Starting over the door, and going to the right, they show: Touch, Hearing, Taste, Scent and Sight. The opening lines of the 1634 entertainment 'Love's Welcome' suggest that it might have started in this room (see page 39). William's arms on the chimney piece show him as Viscount Mansfield, so it dates from no earlier than 1620. The Gothick windows are the work of the vicar John Hamilton Gray, who moved into the Little Castle in 1829.

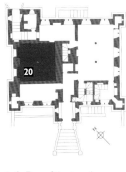

Ground floor

Left: Two of the panels depicting the five senses, Tactus (touch) and Auditus (hearing)
Below left: The Pillar Parlour, which William Cavendish and his guests used as a dining room
Below: John Smythson's drawing of the great chamber panelling at Theobalds Palace, made during a visit to London in 1618, inspired the design of the panelling in the Pillar Parlour

Right: The Star Chamber, with the canopy of state flanked by doors to the stairs to Cavendish's bedchamber (left) and the Marble Closet (right)

21 Star Chamber

The Star Chamber was the great chamber of the Little Castle – a formal reception and dining room, light and airy in contrast to the vaulted spaces below. Its name comes from the gilded lead stars on the sky-blue background of the ceiling, which was painted using blue verditer pigment, a by-product of silver-refining.

The two window walls are elaborately panelled and decorated with paintings of figures from the Old and New Testaments. The windows all originally had shutters, of which a few survive. The images of male saints on the panelling have some similarities to early 16th-century engravings by Marcantonio Raimondi, but none of them can be related to specific prints. The full-length paintings depict the prophet Moses with his tablets, dated 1621, King David, King Solomon and the prophet Aaron, providing religious 'gravitas' for this formal room, while contemporary and playful details, such as the two men in armour and a (lost) image of a boy and cat, are surprising, and bring the scheme to life.

Above: The walls in the Star
Chamber are decorated with
figures from the Old and
New Testaments, such as
King David (top) and King
Solomon (bottom)

When the room was in use, the plain grey painted panelling would have been covered with tapestries or hangings, as it is now, so these walls would actually have appeared richer than the window walls. The tapestries here are reproductions of a mid 17th-century set at Blickling Hall, Norfolk, woven at Mortlake and depicting the story of Abraham. The biblical theme ties in with the religious iconography of the wall-paintings. Modern rush matting reflects the likely original covering of most of the upper floors. Here 'the lord keepeth his presence, and the eyes of all the best sort of strangers be there lookers on', beneath a canopy of state hung for the occasion (see page 22).

The room also emphasizes William's lineage. The frieze at the top of the wall includes the arms of Charles Cavendish and his wife, Katherine Ogle, and their son William and his wife Elizabeth Basset, while the fireplace includes the arms of William's grandmother's last, and most noble, husband, George Talbot, 6th Earl of Shrewsbury.

Cutaway reconstruction
drawing of the Little
Castle in about 1630
A Wardrobe
B Second best
  bedchamber
C Closet
D Star Chamber
E Marble Closet
F Pillar Parlour
G Anteroom
H Kitchen
I Servery
J Entrance stair from
  the forecourt
K Fountain Garden
L Leaded flat roof
M Wall-walk
N Bathhouse, entered
  through the south lodge

22 Marble Closet

This was the withdrawing room, unusually not connected to the route to the best bedchamber. While it was part of Charles Cavendish's plan from the outset, the exceptionally rich marble interior, as well as the French doors and balcony, were created for William in the very latest style. Smythson's initial design exists for a room of this type but with the square plan and including the chimney piece of the Elysium Closet. The height required for the vault, however, was only available here.

The sensual figures in the lunettes are personifications of the Virtues in pastoral settings, after engravings by Hendrick Goltzius of *The United Virtues* of about 1582. They are Fortitude and Patience; Hope and Faith; and Justice and Prudence. Concordia and Peace are absent. Rich hangings covered the plain panelling. Around 1670 these were of 'Cremmson taffetie', and the withdrawing room was furnished in the contemporary fashion with '2 backt chares, 2 Couches with taffity quilts, 1 pittur, 2 Stands, 1 Table; 1 looking Glas'.

First floor

Left: John Smythson's initial design for a marble closet
Below left: Fortitude and Patience *in the Marble Closet, shown with the source engraving by Hendrick Goltzius, c.1582 (bottom)*
Below: The Marble Closet, with the newly restored French doors

First floor

Right: William's bedchamber, with the stool closet door in the corner. The bed would have stood against the wall to the right

23 William's bedchamber

William's bedchamber is reached by a stair from the Star Chamber. Its ceiling is lower, since it is set over the tall vaulted hall. The bed would have been placed against the south wall of the room. The wall-panelling by the window is grained, with gold stencilling, which was uncovered in 1999 from beneath layers of later paint. The rest of the room is painted grey as a background for '3 pieces of

tappistre hangings', mentioned in the 1670s inventory, which would have been similar to the ones in the Star Chamber. The large number of open cupboards, here lined with panelling, would once have been obscured by the tapestries. There are four closets opening off the bedchamber: a stool closet; a dark closet (not open to the public), which was perhaps a wardrobe, originally without a door, so it would have been closed only by the

Right: John Smythson's design for the hall chimney piece, almost as executed in 1616, compared with a design by Serlio (below)

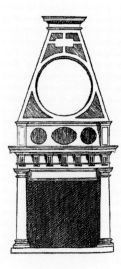

The Fireplaces in the Little Castle

'Chimneys of th'touchstone of affection made,
Therein is beauty, as love's fuel, laid.'
Margaret Cavendish, wife of William Cavendish

The fireplaces in the Little Castle are exquisite, miniature masterpieces, made from local stones including pink alabaster, black touch (Ashford marble) and speckled cockleshell marble. All are variations on a theme, with a projecting panelled stone hood variously supported on columns, pilasters and console brackets. John Smythson designed the first of them in 1616 for Charles Cavendish's hall, in plain limestone. This was inspired by published designs for fireplaces 'in the Italian Style' by the Franco-Italian architect Sebastiano Serlio (1475–1554), but Smythson integrated Gothic motifs with the classical. He developed the concept in richer materials for William, whose coronet and arms as Viscount Mansfield appear on the Pillar Parlour fireplace.

tapestries; and the Heaven and Elysium Closets, with their contrasting visions of the Christian and pagan paradise, divine love compared with licentious sensuality. These were the most private spaces of the suite, into which only the most privileged would have been invited.

24 Heaven Closet

The Heaven Closet takes the form of a cabinet, with cupboards perhaps intended to display and protect precious artefacts or secure personal papers. The panelling is richly decorated with pastoral scenes in gold. It was cut down to accommodate a ceiling painting of the Ascension, dated 1619. This shows angels surrounding the ascending figure of Christ, while the cherubim on the walls hold instruments of the Passion. The subject matter, with its Catholic associations despite William's professed ambivalence in religious matters, could have been inspired by his travels on the Continent.

First floor

Left: The Heaven Closet, a cabinet, which perhaps served as William's study
Below left: The ceiling in the Heaven Closet showing the Ascension of Christ into Heaven
Below: Detail of a cherub from the ceiling of the Heaven Closet. The music is a song about Robin Hood, alluding to William's nostalgia for 'Old England' and the importance he attached to woods and forests. In 1641 he was appointed warden of Sherwood Forest

First floor

Right: The Elysium Closet, which William probably used for intimate social gatherings; the frieze shows the Roman god Bacchus holding a wine bowl aloft, representing liberation and fertility, while Diana (right), associated with virginity, turns away in defeat

25 Elysium Closet

The Elysium Closet was perhaps used for intimate social gatherings. It has French doors (recently reinstated) opening onto a balcony overlooking the Fountain Garden. The balcony in its present form is part of William's completion of Charles's building, but the stone balustrade was not replaced with an iron railing (like the one outside the Marble Closet) until the 1660s. The ceiling depicts the mythological Olympians. The composition and the figure of Minerva derive from an engraving by Cornelius Cort, after a design by the Italian artist Francesco Primaticcio (1504–70) for a ceiling at Fontainebleau. Like the paintings in the Heaven

Closet, these are exceptional survivals from the 17th century in England. The painted sequence seems to end with the banner over the French doors: 'All is But vanitie'. This is the preacher's subject in Ecclesiastes (1:2) that all the wealth and pleasures of this world are meaningless or futile; satisfaction comes only through faith in God, perhaps a direction away from sensual pagan pleasure (Bacchus flanked by naked followers is prominent in the frieze) and back to Heaven. As in the Heaven Closet, the panelling was cut down to accommodate the paintings. The decoration of the panelling was extravagantly expensive, with an indigo glaze over gesso, marbled with shell gold.

Left: Detail of the banner over the French doors in the Elysium Closet: 'All is But vanitie', from Ecclesiastes 1:2. On the soffit of the arch below the banner are two philosophers contemplating the world, one laughing and the other weeping
Below left: From the right, Minerva, goddess of wisdom, holding her owl; Mercury, the messenger god, with his winged hat; two putti with a peacock, identifying the next figure as Juno, protector of marriage, looking away from her unfaithful consort, Jupiter

The Wall-paintings at Bolsover

An exceptional survival from the early 17th century

Painted decoration had been used on the walls of fashionable English houses since medieval times. Around the time the Little Castle was completed by William Cavendish, however, the fashion was changing away from decorative, repeating patterns to figurative scenes. William's choices reflected the latest taste in London and at Court.

Like plasterers and woodcarvers, the painters usually adapted scenes from their stock of continental, particularly Flemish, prints of biblical, mythological or allegorical subjects. The iconographic schemes, however, were usually the result of a collaboration between painter and patron, who might himself contribute source material. Many of the paintings at Bolsover fit this pattern, but the ceilings of the Heaven and Elysium closets seem to be influenced by rather than directly copied from prints. Some of the figures in Elysium are painted in sophisticated poses yet are awkwardly related to each other, suggesting that they have been plucked out of other contexts.

The figure of Minerva, for example, was taken from a published design by Francesco Primaticcio, which seems to have inspired the general composition.

Primaticcio was trained by Giulio Romano, and so provides an artistic link between Elysium and Romano's decoration of the Hall of Psyche in the Palazzo del Te in Mantua. It is possible that William paid a fleeting visit to Mantua in 1612 but his commissioning of horse portraits (see page 6) and portraits of the Caesars is as likely to be due to the purchase of the Mantua originals by Charles I in 1628.

Decorative painters were organized like skilled tradesmen, most being members of the London livery company of Painter-Stainers. Men such as Rowland Buckett (1572–1639), the most successful decorative painter of his time, employed assistants and took on apprentices in his workshop. We do not know who painted the pictures at Bolsover, but stylistic differences suggest that several painters from more than one workshop were involved.

Above: The lantern on the top floor, with stone seats between the arches and a raised stone floor. William Cavendish's guests might have taken dessert here

Right: The chimney piece in William's mother's room, described as 'the roome that gives light to Hardwik'

26 Nursery

The inventory of about 1670 suggests that this room was then called the 'Nurssey' and contained a bed, a table and five stools. This is consistent with the simple decoration and chimney piece, which is similar to those in the anteroom and the passage on the floor below. The name probably dates back to the 1620s and 1630s when William's children were young. The boarded floor and the window seat date from the late 18th century.

27 Second Floor

The focal point of the top floor is the central lantern – the architectural *tour de force* of the house – a place to sit and perhaps to take dessert. The elaborate fireplaces and panelling testify to the high status of the upper-floor rooms. The larger ones were bedchambers, as large or larger than William's bedchamber and similarly decorated. The largest, at the north-west corner, was probably William's mother's room and in about 1670 it was called 'the roome that gives light to Hardwik', that is to say, it was visible from Hardwick and Hardwick could be seen from it. The smaller unheated rooms were called 'closits', but contained beds. The plain unheated room on the north side was probably the wardrobe, where hangings and linen were stored when not in use.

The great stair continued upwards to give Cavendish and his guests access to the original flat-leaded roof. This floor now appears much plainer than it was because the roof structure was replaced in 1750. The plaster cornices were removed and rough plaster ceilings were inserted throughout the top floor. The loss of panelling probably began about the same time.

28 Basement

As in the Terrace Range, there was originally no connection between the kitchens and cellars at basement level, which is why there are three internal and two external sets of stairs. At the bottom of the back stair is the servery, where food drawn through hatches from the kitchen and pastry was assembled. It was also where supplies were brought in from the forecourt, with access to two levels of larder under the porch as well as to the dark fuel store. The upper larder off the stair has 'Cheese Room' painted on the door, suggesting it was the original dairy larder. A room

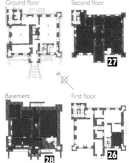

Ground floor | Second floor

27

Basement | First floor

28 | 26

Left: The kitchen looking towards the entrance and serving hatch. The bench and shelf are typical of 17th- and 18th-century kitchen fittings
Below left: The bank of pastry ovens. A fire of twigs was lit in an open oven, and the embers were raked out into the small openings at floor level before the food was inserted and the door shut
Below right: Detail of a 17th-century kitchen from the painting Outside the Kitchen *by David Teniers, 1680*

in a house, designated for storing cheese, was exempt from the window tax, imposed between 1696 and 1851.

The pastry has a bank of three ovens opening from a single firing point, a design copied in the Terrace Range. It also has its own warm, dry store alongside. The kitchen has two fireplaces – the left one for roasting, the other for boiling and a stove. It remained in use into the 1880s, although by then the wet larder beyond, with its stone salting vats, seems to have been used as the scullery.

The kitchen seems to have been first linked to the cellars in the late 17th century, through the blocked door by the fireplace. The wine cellars

were connected to the high end of the hall by the small stair opposite the door to the external stair, through which drink was brought in. The great beer cellar would have had barrels set on timber racks.

Right: Venus on top of her fountain, with the western garden room in the background

Below: View of the Venus Garden in the 1630s, with a round bowl to the fountain. This series of drawings is generally accurate, so the present basin could be a late change of design, possibly created for the royal visit of 1634. Otherwise, little has changed in this view other than the stone balustrade to the balcony, replaced in iron after about 1660

ⓑ WALL-WALK AND FOUNTAIN GARDEN

When the Little Castle was built, the inner ward of the medieval castle became its garden. The surrounding great wall was adapted and refaced to provide an elevated walk called the 'High Walke' in the 17th century, which opens off the great stair of the Little Castle. The doorway was greatly embellished in about 1633, when a bridge link was

first created to the chapel in the newly completed Terrace Range. The garden's centrepiece, the Venus Fountain, designed by John Smythson, probably marked the completion of this campaign before the royal visit of 1634. In this very rare survival, Venus is depicted emerging from her bath, holding a cloth, after a statue in Florence by Giambologna. The present basin, with busts of Roman emperors in the niches and lustful mythical beasts on platforms at the angles, could be a late change of design.

The Little Castle garden has recently been replanted with period plants, using evidence from 17th-century garden writers such as John Gerard and John Parkinson in his book *Paradisi in Sole Paradisus Terrestris* (1629). Gardeners were interested in unusual varieties of plants, which would have provided colour and interest throughout the growing season. The present gravel garden is inspired by Gervase Markham's description in *The English Husbandman* (1613) of temporary gardens, which could be cut from the turf and decorated with coloured soils and gravel.

ⓒ Garden Rooms

The garden could also be entered through a wide gateway on the west (later blocked), adjoining a rib-vaulted garden room probably fitted with largely glazed doors, which have now been reinstated. This was most likely used for banqueting and is connected to an inner, vaulted room; they have Smythson-designed fireplaces for cooler days. Both rooms were created within a thickening of the wall. Across the garden are seats alternating with niches, which would have been used for beehives or possibly lanterns. In contrast, the two small rooms on the opposite side of the garden are utilitarian vaulted chambers with large plain fireplaces. One was probably the still house, used for distilling medicines and spirits. The other room could have been the chamber in which William and his chaplain, Dr Robert Payne, conducted chemical experiments. On examining the properties of a compound of brimstone and saltpetre, for example, Cavendish surmised that the sun 'is nothing but a very solid body of salt and sulphur, inflamed by its own motion upon its own axis'. William is also known to have corresponded with the mathematician and philosopher René Descartes (1596–1650) and other 17th-century intellectuals.

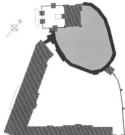

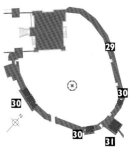

31 Cistern House

Water for the castle was collected at the Cundy House on the east side of the Hockley valley, and from there it was siphoned across the valley to the cistern house, which stands in the angle between

the outer and inner court walls (another supply came in from the south, along the terrace). The interior structure of the cistern house now dates from the 19th century, but in the 17th century water was pumped up from siphon level to a lantern on the roof above the wall-walk, to supply the fountain. The middle level, rebuilt in the 1630s, housed a comfortable heated room with large windows overlooking a Wilderness on the side of the valley. This room and the Wilderness were both reached from the great court by stairs around the outside of the building.

The Fountain Garden and great court walls were seriously damaged by the Commonwealth forces, to prevent the castle being held against them (see page 41), and they were only repaired after William Cavendish returned from exile in 1660. Having decided that the great court would become the focus of his new buildings rather than primarily a service area, he shifted the main garden gate to the south, onto the axis of the new riding house. His new great court wall incorporated a rusticated doorway that led to a platform overlooking the Wilderness. The bridge to the Terrace Range was rebuilt, incorporating a new bathhouse below (not open to the public).

CAVENDISH FAMILY TREE

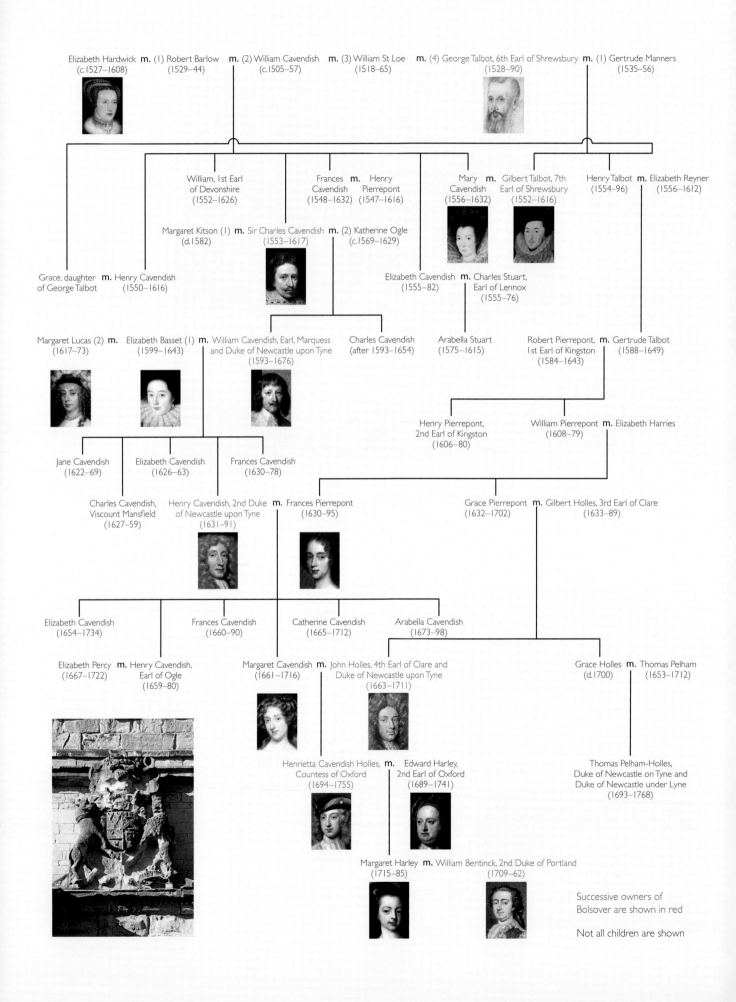

Elizabeth Hardwick **m.** (1) Robert Barlow (c.1527–1608) (1529–44) **m.** (2) William Cavendish (c.1505–57) **m.** (3) William St Loe (1518–65) **m.** (4) George Talbot, 6th Earl of Shrewsbury (1528–90) **m.** (1) Gertrude Manners (1535–56)

William, 1st Earl of Devonshire (1552–1626)

Frances Cavendish (1548–1632) **m.** Henry Pierrepont (1547–1616)

Mary Cavendish (1556–1632) **m.** Gilbert Talbot, 7th Earl of Shrewsbury (1552–1616)

Henry Talbot (1554–96) **m.** Elizabeth Reyner (1556–1612)

Margaret Kitson (1) **m.** Sir Charles Cavendish (d.1582) (1553–1617) **m.** (2) Katherine Ogle (c.1569–1629)

Grace, daughter of George Talbot **m.** Henry Cavendish (1550–1616)

Elizabeth Cavendish (1555–82) **m.** Charles Stuart, Earl of Lennox (1555–76)

Margaret Lucas (2) **m.** (1617–73)

Elizabeth Basset (1) **m.** (1599–1643)

William Cavendish, Earl, Marquess and Duke of Newcastle upon Tyne (1593–1676)

Charles Cavendish (after 1593–1654)

Arabella Stuart (1575–1615)

Robert Pierrepont, 1st Earl of Kingston (1584–1643) **m.** Gertrude Talbot (1588–1649)

Henry Pierrepont, 2nd Earl of Kingston (1606–80)

William Pierrepont (1608–79) **m.** Elizabeth Harries

Jane Cavendish (1622–69)

Elizabeth Cavendish (1626–63)

Frances Cavendish (1630–78)

Charles Cavendish, Viscount Mansfield (1627–59)

Henry Cavendish, 2nd Duke of Newcastle upon Tyne (1631–91) **m.** Frances Pierrepont (1630–95)

Grace Pierrepont (1632–1702) **m.** Gilbert Holles, 3rd Earl of Clare (1633–89)

Elizabeth Cavendish (1654–1734)

Frances Cavendish (1660–90)

Catherine Cavendish (1665–1712)

Arabella Cavendish (1673–98)

Elizabeth Percy (1667–1722) **m.** Henry Cavendish, Earl of Ogle (1659–80)

Margaret Cavendish (1661–1716) **m.** John Holles, 4th Earl of Clare and Duke of Newcastle upon Tyne (1663–1711)

Grace Holles (d.1700) **m.** Thomas Pelham (1653–1712)

Henrietta Cavendish Holles, Countess of Oxford (1694–1755) **m.** Edward Harley, 2nd Earl of Oxford (1689–1741)

Thomas Pelham-Holles, Duke of Newcastle on Tyne and Duke of Newcastle under Lyne (1693–1768)

Margaret Harley **m.** William Bentinck, 2nd Duke of Portland (1715–85) (1709–62)

Successive owners of Bolsover are shown in red

Not all children are shown

History

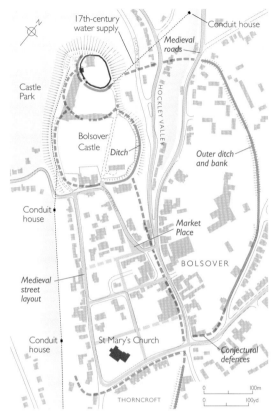

THE MEDIEVAL CASTLE

In 1068 William the Conqueror (r.1066–87) granted custody of his new castle at Nottingham to one of his knights, William Peveril (c.1040–1114), together with extensive estates in the area. These included the large manor of Bolsover, which extended from the meadows along the river Doe Lea to the west to the arable fields and commons of the plateau to the east. By 1086 Peveril had built a castle at Castleton in Derbyshire; he probably built Bolsover soon afterwards.

Surviving earthworks and some evidence from excavation show that the early castle took the form of an inner court and bailey at the end of the promontory, corresponding approximately to the Fountain Garden and great court (see plan, page 3). The inner court was walled early – the polygonal plan resembling that at Nottingham Castle. The pre-Conquest manor and church seem to have survived just to the south-east of the castle, until engulfed in a large outer bailey (the castle yard), around the turn of the 11th and 12th centuries. Probably at the same time, an enclosed

settlement was laid out beyond the castle gate, and the church was moved to its present site, within it. Substantial earthworks still define the settlement. Like Bolsover, Castleton also has extensive earthworks, but it is uncertain whether either originated before Peveril's son, also William, finally forfeited his estates to the Crown in 1155, having taken the wrong side against Henry II.

The Crown garrisoned Bolsover Castle, and under successive monarchs it was embellished, repaired and rebuilt, notably after a siege during the First Barons' War in 1216, when a group of barons fought against King John (r.1199–1216), because he refused to accept the terms of the Magna Carta. Wall-towers were added or rebuilt during the 13th century and references in accounts show that the castle had a set of king's and queen's lodgings, probably in and between the towers of the inner court, one of which was the great tower. The garrison was finally stood down in 1322 and from then on the buildings gradually fell into decay. For more than two centuries, the manor and castle were let to tenants. None of them is known to have lived at Bolsover but some buildings were perhaps kept habitable for a steward.

CHARLES CAVENDISH AND THE CREATION OF THE LITTLE CASTLE

George Talbot, later 6th Earl of Shrewsbury, bought the manor of Bolsover from the Crown in 1553. In 1567 he married Elizabeth ('Bess') Hardwick and the following year her daughter Mary married George's second son, Gilbert, who inherited as 7th Earl in 1590 (see family tree opposite). Bess's youngest son, Charles (from her earlier marriage to Sir William Cavendish), bought Welbeck Abbey from Gilbert as his principal residence in 1600. He took a lease of Bolsover in 1608, acquiring the freehold of the manor and six adjacent manors in 1613. There was already a small, habitable 'old house' at the castle. This had probably been built or rebuilt during the Talbot ownership and stood on the site of the northern part of the Terrace Range.

Charles Cavendish was a soldier by profession, with a passion for music, the arts and architecture.

Left: A plan of medieval Bolsover, showing the town, which was granted a market in 1226, set within a large enclosure to the south of the castle, following the escarpment, with another enclosure of unknown but later date and purpose to the east

Above: George Talbot, 6th Earl of Shrewsbury, who bought the manor of Bolsover from the Crown in 1553

Facing page bottom: The arms of William Cavendish as Duke of Newcastle, from the entrance to the state apartment

He was influenced no doubt by his mother's extensive and innovative building at her Derbyshire houses, Chatsworth, Hardwick and Oldcotes. As well as building for himself at Welbeck, Charles devised house plans for other members of his circle, using a draughtsman to make fair copies.

Designing the Little Castle

Cultivated and with ample funds, Charles was keen to make his mark at Bolsover. Surviving building accounts show that he started to build the Little Castle over the winter of 1611–12, in anticipation of acquiring the freehold. Work began by 'making a way into the castle' (presumably the origin of the terrace) and setting up a lime kiln on site and masons' lodges at the quarries. The cellars were dug and a section of the 'great wall' of the inner court of the medieval castle was removed. Part of the base of this wall survives beneath the forecourt. The foundations of the Little Castle were begun on 30 March 1612.

Drawings by John Smythson for the basement and the hall chimney piece survive, closely resembling what was built, and he was clearly the 'Mr Smithson' who oversaw the work documented in the 1612–13 accounts. Given Charles's knowledge and experience as a patron, however, the design is likely to have been the result of a creative partnership between him, John and possibly John's elderly father, Robert.

The Little Castle followed the characteristic form of a lodge, tall and positioned to take advantage of the views yet intimate and self-contained – a place for retreat and pleasure. Seen from the forecourt, its expanse of windows and symmetrical façade look almost conventional for the time, with some resemblances to Hardwick. But from a distance, its austere form dominates, rising sheer from the cliff. It is a clear evocation of a Norman great tower, modernized through the centuries. As the younger son of upwardly mobile parents, but now married to an heiress, Katherine, 8th Baroness Ogle, Charles Cavendish was keen to evoke an ancient lineage through the architecture of the Little Castle. So successful was the design that the myth of the Little Castle actually being a Norman tower persisted into the 20th century.

The interior convincingly continues the conceit, with massive round Romanesque vaults in the basement and pointed Gothic ones on the entrance floor. The great windows of the upper floors are designed to give panoramic views across the landscape, even though this meant that the principal rooms all faced west or north.

Completing the Structure

Cavendish was evidently an old man in a hurry. While a thatcher began to cover the wall heads for the winter at the end of the normal building season in October 1612, work on some of the cellar vaults continued, probably under temporary cover. The wet larder pillar was set just before Christmas and work continued on the vault into February 1613. Although accounts survive only for the first year and a half, the pace of work is consistent with the structure of the castle and forecourt being complete by the time Charles died on 4 April 1617. By then, the fitting out of the interior was in hand, with the hall chimney piece dated 1616. It was left to Charles's eldest son, William, to finish the Little Castle.

Robert and John Smythson

Skilled designers with a personal style

The Renaissance idea of an architect as an educated, independent designer of classical buildings, a man of some social standing, was slow to develop in England. Before the Restoration in 1660, most important buildings emerged from a creative partnership between client and master-builder. The Smythsons were among those, usually masons, who developed as skilled designers with a personal style.

Robert Smythson

Robert (1535–1614) first appears in 1568 as a master mason for Sir John Thynne, at Longleat House in Wiltshire. In his next commission, modernizing the medieval Old Wardour Castle, Wiltshire, he probably came to appreciate the architectural potential of tall, compact houses. Robert came to the Midlands in about 1580, now as 'Mr Smythson', to be 'Architecter and Surveyor unto the most worthy house of Wollaton with divers others of great account', as his funerary monument records, probably making use of Sir Francis Willoughby's extensive library of continental architectural books at Wollaton. He remained at Wollaton for the rest of his life, as bailiff to the Willoughbys. He also designed other tall houses in the region, including the now-lost Worksop Manor for George Talbot, 6th Earl of Shrewsbury, and probably Hardwick New Hall for the earl's second wife, Bess.

John Smythson

Robert's son John (c.1560s–1634) also trained as a mason and is first recorded working for his father at Wollaton in 1588. His later career reflected his father's; from about 1612 he was bailiff to Charles Cavendish, and later to William. In his will he calls himself 'Architectur' with a 'Library and Books', designing for other clients as well as for the Cavendish family. His architectural style drew on lively, often exaggerated ('Mannerist') versions of classicism, which had become rooted in the culture of the region. The court style of Inigo Jones, parodied in 'Love's Welcome' (see page 39) by the character of 'Coronell Iniquo Vitruvius', in contrast, was based on Roman classicism, following rules of proportion inspired by Vitruvius.

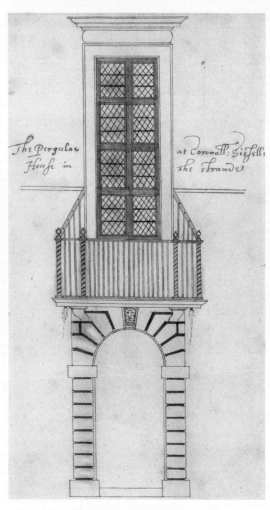

The Pergulae House in *at Coronell: Sissell, the strande*

Above: *Wollaton Hall, Nottingham, built between 1580 and 1588 to the design of Robert Smythson*
Left: *The 'pergola' at Col Sissell's house in the Strand, drawn by John Smythson on a visit to London in 1618. The French doors and the green-painted iron balustrade were used on the front of the Little Castle, but with a much more elaborate doorcase*

Above: William Cavendish performing 'Ballotades par le Droite', an engraving from his book on horsemanship, published in 1658, with the Little Castle as a backdrop
Right: William's first wife, Elizabeth Basset, painted by William Larkin on her marriage in 1618

WILLIAM CAVENDISH

William inherited at the age of 25, and in the following year, 1618, married a Staffordshire heiress, Elizabeth Basset. As a young man he had travelled to northern Italy with the diplomat Sir Henry Wotton (1568–1639) and been impressed by the etiquette of the Court of Savoy. The trip gave him a cultural tour of Europe, through France, on to the Court of Savoy at Turin and home via Milan, Basle and the Rhine valley. His first biographer, his second wife, Margaret, paints a picture of a cultured man, with an inherited love of music, poetry and architecture, who was equally fond of swordsmanship and 'heroic actions'. Seemingly a great philanderer, but at the same time a loving husband to his two successive wives, he was fond of fashion and magnificence rather than business. Above all, he spent his time in 'principally horses of all sorts, but more particularly, horses of *manège*', finding comfort in the discipline of horsemanship (see page 5). William was first ennobled in 1620 as Viscount Mansfield and in 1628 was created Earl of Newcastle upon Tyne.

Virtually no direct documentary evidence survives for William's work at Bolsover before the mid 1660s, let alone anything about his intentions underlying it. Our understanding of the sequence of buildings and William's architectural and decorative choices is based on the evidence embodied in the buildings themselves, contemporary and early descriptions and literary allusions, topographic sketches from the 1630s, and a small number of John Smythson's design drawings that testify to the continuation of the creative partnership between designer and patron. While the chronological sequence is generally clear, its absolute dating is less certain, and the interpretation of the function of different rooms, their sources and William's motivation is to varying extents speculative.

Finishing the Little Castle

William completed the decoration of his father's lodge house by about 1621, inspired in part by buildings in or near London, drawn at William's request by John Smythson when they visited the capital over the winter of 1618–19: 'for Bolsover furneshinge, payntinge & carving will be better thought off att London then heer', wrote William.

The sculpture and paintings are mostly adaptations of European prints of biblical and

Left: The Little Castle from the forecourt, drawn in the 1630s. This is part of a set of drawings, whose artist is unknown, that provided the source for the backdrops to the illustrations in William Cavendish's book; its counterpart appears opposite
Below: Wall-painting in the hall of the Little Castle, depicting Hercules stealing the mares of Diomedes. The scene is set in a painted extension of the hall vaulting, to create the illusion that the figures are in the room

classical images with metaphorical or symbolic meaning. Except for the Heaven and Elysium Closets, the subjects of many of the paintings in the Little Castle are all common Renaissance themes and demonstrate William's sophistication and cultural breadth. Some have interpreted the iconography of the Little Castle as an allegory of reconciling human weakness, or vanity, as depicted in the Elysium Closet, with the desire to go to Heaven, seeing the wall-paintings as a reflection of the Neo-Platonist philosophical idea of the universe as a series of layers leading upwards towards divine love. The sensual nature of many of the paintings, however, suggests that William Cavendish had rather more earthly love on his mind. The subject matter of the paintings in the Elysium and Marble Closets suited their use as private withdrawing spaces, while the religious iconography in the Star Chamber was appropriate for its use as the main room for formal entertaining.

Building the Terrace Range

Between 1622 and 1625, Cavendish was busy remodelling his principal house at Welbeck. He built his first riding house and a great stable at Welbeck, both to John Smythson's design, before turning his attention to the 'old house' at Bolsover, on the site of the Terrace Range. His original aim appears to have been to rebuild it with a long, 11-bay elevation facing out across the vale, entered at first-floor level from the terrace, but otherwise rather conservative in its design. Only the scale of the kitchens and cellars suggests that it was designed primarily for large-scale entertainment.

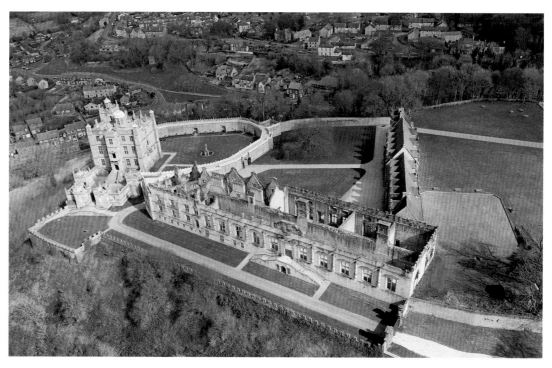

Above: Miniature portrait of William Cavendish, c.1650s

Right: Aerial view of Bolsover from the south-west. The stair marks the centre of the gallery of about 1630, whose scale contrasts with the domestic spaces of the northern end of the Terrace Range, carried over from the mid 1620s design

Below: A ground-floor plan by John Smythson of about 1630 for adding a state apartment and gallery to the half-built first version of the Terrace Range, whose centre is marked by the door to 'The Passage' at the left-hand end (see page 15)

Once the building work had reached first-floor level, there was a hiatus and a dramatic change of plan. A very large state apartment, backed by a gallery, was interlocked with the south end of the Terrace Range; the architectural collision is clear in a 1630s drawing (see page 15). Smythson's plan for this reworking survives and includes a chapel across the southern end, which was not built. One was created instead on the top floor of the north end of the Terrace Range, marked on the outside by geometric gables and lantern finials. It was accessed from the wall-walk by a doorway, dated 1633.

This change of plan was probably prompted by William's ambitions at court, and facilitated by the Ogle inheritance, following his mother's death in 1629. The range had now become something

unique in England: a freestanding state apartment and gallery with only a hall, service rooms and a few modest lodgings attached. It seems reasonable to conclude that its primary purpose was to impress and accommodate King Charles I (r.1625–49), who visited Welbeck briefly in 1633 on his way to Scotland and returned the following year to Welbeck and Bolsover with Queen Henrietta Maria. The building would have evoked the idea of an Italian Mannerist palazzo set above terraced gardens on an English hill, although at this stage it was still architecturally rather incoherent. The investment (or gamble) was eventually to pay off. Four years after the magnificent entertainment of 1634, William achieved his objective of being appointed governor to Charles, Prince of Wales, although he only managed to hold the post until 1641.

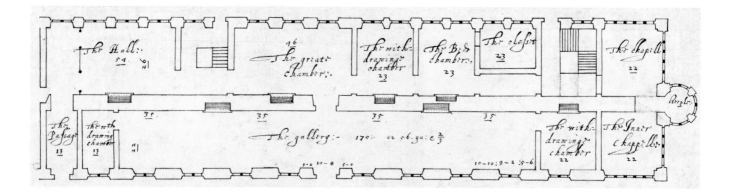

The Royal Visit and 'Love's Welcome'

On 30 July 1634, Charles I and Henrietta Maria visited Bolsover for a lavish entertainment.

A royal progress was an occasion for the hosts to impress through magnificent display, in the hope of obtaining or retaining a position at Court. It was also an opportunity for the king and queen to present themselves before the local gentry, in order to encourage their loyalty. On their progress in 1634, King Charles I and Queen Henrietta Maria stayed several days at Welbeck. On 30 July the royal entourage came over to Bolsover for a lavish feast and entertainment, 'Love's Welcome', devised by Ben Jonson, to which all the gentry of Nottinghamshire and Derbyshire were invited.

The surviving texts of the entertainment begin with a welcoming 'song at the banquet', the serving of sweetmeats, fruit and wine, which would normally follow the meal:

> 'If Love be called a Lifting of the Sense
> To Knowledge of that pure Intelligence
> Wherein the soule hath rest and residence?
>
> Where were the Senses in such order plac'd?
> The Sight; the Heareing, Smelling, Touching, Tast?
> All at one banquet? would it ever last'

Charles and Henrietta Maria then 'retir'd into a garden', presumably the Fountain Garden, to be entertained by dancers dressed as building tradesmen, led by their 'Survayour' Coronell Iniquo Vitruvius, urging them to 'Use Holiday Leggs and have 'hem Spring, Leape, Caper and gingle', to a tune played by the blacksmith. Next 'The King and Queene, having repos'd themselves at their departure in a fitt place', 'a second Banquet [was] set downe before them from the Cloudes by two Loves'. The cupids Eros and Anteros, love and love reciprocated, charmingly complete each other's compliments before a philosopher praises the royal couple as the very personification of love. It is not clear where this theatrical staging took place: perhaps elsewhere in the garden or in the great chamber in the newly built Terrace Range. The entertainment would have been fabulous – an extravagant spectacle of costume, dance,

music and theatre, following a feast at which 41 species of bird were eaten, including 30 swans, 30 peacocks, 30 turkeys, 40 herons, 10 dozen geese and nearly 600 domestic fowl, as well as numerous smaller birds, such as larks and redshanks.

After his entertainment of the king at Welbeck in the previous year, Cavendish complained that 'I have hurt the estate much with the hopes' of obtaining high office at Court. But the 1634 visit and entertainment were much more lavish, costing the equivalent of a year's rental from Cavendish's estates.

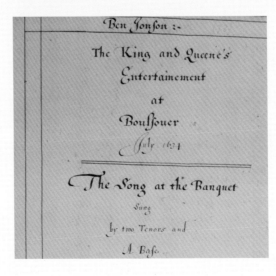

Above: The Garden of Love *by Peter Paul Rubens, painted in about 1633 as an allegory of conjugal love, with the artist and his young wife as the focus. The idealized garden, like Bolsover, has Mannerist classical architecture and a statue of Venus in the background, as well as cupids hovering against clouds. There was a copy of this painting 'after Rubens' in the Cavendish collection at Welbeck Abbey*

Left: The opening page of a manuscript of 'Love's Welcome', written by Ben Jonson and performed at Bolsover in 1634*

Trouble with the Lead Miners

On the day of the royal visit in 1634, a group of miners was marching towards Bolsover and Welbeck to protest about tithes on mining.

Ben Jonson's play for the entertainment of 1634 proclaimed love and harmony in a well-ordered hierarchical society, but the reality beyond the gates was rather different. On the day of the performance, the king's secretary Sir John Coke wrote from Welbeck to William Cavendish at Bolsover, to inform him that 'a great multitude of Miners assemble them selues at Baslowe to cum tomorrow morning to your howse & present unto [the king] a mutinous petition which is not sufferable in a wel governed state'. The king commanded Cavendish as Lord Lieutenant of Derbyshire to muster the trained bands (local militia) and 'prohibite & scatter such assemblie & to apprehend & imprison the chief authors thereof… to suppress this tumult that their Maiesties may receave euey honor you intend them without distraction'.

Lead mining in the Derbyshire Peak was nominally controlled by the Crown, rather than by the manorial landowners. Free miners had ancient rights to take lead from land in the 'King's Field' subject only to the payment of royalties to the Crown and tithes to the Church. After the Reformation, the Crown leased the tithes to laymen. Both the great landowners and the miners resented the tithe and sought to abolish it, while the Cavendish family had tried to prove that some of their manors were exempt from the freedom of the 'King's Field'. The protest of July 1634 was provoked by the Dowager Countess of Devonshire (rather than the miners themselves) acquiring the right to the tithes through the duplicity of the king's attorney-general Sir Robert Heath, whom the miners thought was acting for them. He also collected Crown royalties on lead in the manor of Wirksworth. The custom that the monarch on progress should accept petitions from his subjects was well established, yet the miners were in effect treated as rebels, 'kept back by force', and their leaders, mostly small landowners, confined in gaol at Derby until the winter. These events reflect the tensions in society and the increasing political organization of the population in the years before the Civil War.

THE CIVIL WAR

Charles I and Archbishop Laud wanted to unite the English and Scottish Churches and imposed a series of reforms on the Scots. They were violently opposed to what they saw as a threat to their national identity and signed the Scottish National Covenant in 1638. Despite lacking support at home, adequate funds, or experienced commanders, Charles tried to impose his authority by force. Early in 1639, William Cavendish lent the king £10,000 and rode north with his Prince of Wales Troop of cavalry to join the king's army at Berwick. The campaign ended in a truce; another campaign in the following year ended in defeat at the Battle of Newburn.

In November 1640, William joined the king's Privy Council, and soon after the outbreak of the Civil War in 1642 he was appointed commander-in-chief of the northern Royalist counties. Elevated to Marquess of Newcastle upon Tyne in November 1643, William was at first successful. After returning briefly to Bolsover in April 1643, where his wife Elizabeth lay dying, he came back in December to set up a garrison under Colonel Muschamp; traces of his refortification of the outer bailey defences were found when the visitor centre was built in 1999. But the following year, fighting alongside Prince Rupert, he lost the decisive Battle of Marston Moor on 2 July 1644, which broke the power of the northern Royalists. Despondent, William went into exile on the Continent, first to Hamburg, then to Paris.

On 14 August 1645, Parliamentarian forces under Major-General Crawford began to erect batteries outside the castle. Seeing his position was hopeless, Muschamp surrendered and he and his men were allowed to leave with their horses, small arms and personal possessions.

Bolsover under the Commonwealth

Maintaining Bolsover became a drain on Parliamentary resources and in 1649 the Council of State ordered the slighting of the castle to prevent it being used by Royalists. This included demolition of 'the outworks abroad, and garden walls, with the turrets and walls of the frontier court that are of strength', and the removal of the strong doors and window bars from the house, which 'as it relates to private habitation, may be as little prejudiced as may be'. In April 1650 the castle

Left: Margaret, Duchess of Newcastle, William Cavendish's second wife, by Sir Peter Lely, c.1665
Below: *Detail from a portrait of Charles Cavendish, William Cavendish's brother, who bought back Bolsover and Welbeck after the Civil War and placed them in trust for William's son Henry*

was sold to a speculator, Robert Thorpe, the cost of the demolition to be offset by the value of the building materials.

William remained in exile, marrying Margaret Lucas (see page 43) in Paris in 1645. He subsequently moved to Antwerp, where he rented the Rubenshuis, former home of the artist Peter Paul Rubens. Here he established a riding school, exercised 'the art of *manège*,' and in 1658 he published his first work on horsemanship: *Méthode et invention nouvelle de dresser les chevaux.* Appointed a member of Charles II's Privy Council in exile in 1650, he refused to acknowledge the Commonwealth, choosing, like many other Royalists, to remain abroad until the Restoration in 1660.

The intervention of William's brother, Charles, saved Bolsover. He returned to London in 1650, apologized to the Commonwealth for his role in the war and bought back his own estates, together with Welbeck and Bolsover, which, in 1652, he placed in trust for William's son Henry. He died soon afterwards and William's elder son, also called Charles, moved into Bolsover.

Right: An engraving of Bolsover Castle by Jan Kip after Leonard Knyff, 1698. It gives a good impression of the landscape in front of the castle, with the road from Chesterfield on the left crossing the river Doe Lea, and the former castle park beyond

Below: Part of a 'Plan of the Earl of Newcastle's Lands in the Manor of Bolsover', 1630–37, by William Senior. The purpose of the plan was to map the agricultural land, so the town and castle are shown schematically. The castle yard and great court are visible, but the Little Castle and Fountain Garden are omitted

REBUILDING AFTER THE CIVIL WAR

The Little Castle remained intact through the Civil War, although it had been stripped of its contents. Charles Cavendish, William's elder son, spent £15,14s.4d. on glazing in 1656 and at some point the gateway to the forecourt was rebuilt. On Charles's death in 1659, William's second son, Henry, took over and began to plan work. William wrote on 22 October 1659 asking him to delay 'the alteringe of the Chimneys dors & windowes', but of what we do not know. As well as the garden, great court and 'frontier court' (castle yard) walls, later references and the extent of works suggest that the leaded flat roofs had been stripped from the hall, gallery and state apartment in the Terrace Range. The rebuilding of the state apartment in the mid 1660s suggests that its walls had also suffered major damage. It was probably not considered part of the 'private habitation', but it was an obvious political target.

Re-roofing the Hall

There has been a great deal of debate about the dating of the re-roofing of the hall in the Terrace Range and particularly the building of the Riding House Range, as there is little documentary evidence for this work. It is most likely that a new roof was built over the hall because the original one had been destroyed during the Civil War. Had the original flat roof structure still existed, new garret rooms could much more easily have been constructed on top of it, so adding the rooms is unlikely to have been the driving force

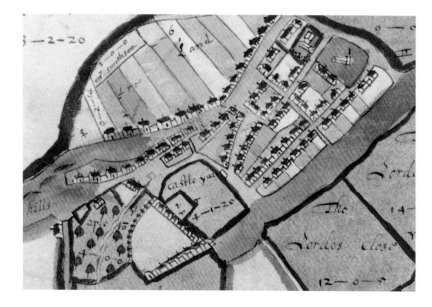

Margaret, Duchess of Newcastle

Margaret Cavendish wanted 'to be known to the world by my wit, not by my folly'.

Margaret Lucas (1623–73) was, by her own account, 'a shy young woman, given to contemplation'. Nevertheless she joined Queen Henrietta Maria's impromptu Court at Oxford during the Civil War, following her into exile in Paris. There she met (and in 1645 married) William Cavendish, who 'did approve of those bashful fears which many condemned, and would choose such a wife as he might bring to his own humours' (disposition).

Margaret's words reflect not the moulding of a compliant young wife, but her introduction as an equal into William's intellectual world, against the conventions of the time. Much has been made of her 'delight in a singularity' (idiosyncracy), wearing extravagant clothes, but her reputation depended on her writing; she wished 'to be known to the world by my wit, not by my folly'. Her output included poetry, drama and one of the earliest science fiction stories (*The Blazing World*, 1668); one of the first secular autobiographies, published in 1656; and a biography of her husband, a vindication of his life, published in 1667. Her interest in and writings on 'natural philosophy' (science) were even more unusual. She was the first woman to be invited to a meeting of the Royal Society, in 1667 (women were afterwards excluded until 1945). In addition to contributing to the discussion of the nature of matter, she helped popularize the 17th-century revolution in scientific thinking through her book *Grounds of Natural Philosophy* (1668). Self-promotion in print and a desire for fame were very much male prerogatives, but Margaret took pride in 'the censures of this age', arguing for the education of women, not least in science.

Once they were back in England, Margaret faced hostility from William's own children and household. In 1670 Andrew Clayton, William's steward, led a conspiracy by his servants, accusing Margaret of adultery and wanting 'to inrich her selfe for a second husband'. But it was all to no avail. After Margaret died in 1673, William committed much of the estate income that would have supported her in widowhood to the building of Nottingham Castle, a gesture that his heir, Henry, much resented.

Left: Margaret at her writing table in her closet, from the frontispiece of her book The World's Olio *(1671), a collection of poems and essays on scientific, historical and philosophical topics*

Below: An imaginary gathering of William and Margaret, William's children and their wives, set in a Dutch interior, from an edition of Margaret Cavendish's collected writings

Above: A version of the lost picture La Bataille Gaignee, which once hung in the gallery at Bolsover (see page 14), from a series of 17th-century tapestries of equestrian figures by Michel Wauters
Below: Portrait of Ben Jonson by Abraham van Blyenberch, c.1617

'When first, my Lord, I saw you back your horse,
Provoke his mettle and command his force …
Nay, so your seat his beauties did endorse,
As I began to wish myself a horse.'
Ben Jonson, writing about William Cavendish, quoted in Cavendish's second treatise on horsemanship (1667)

behind the changes. This work introduced some motifs not previously used at Bolsover: the pedimented scrolled gables (the adjacent straight ones were altered to match the new ones); a new hall fireplace with bold chamfered rustication (see page 10); and, in the garrets, a distinctive simplified form of architrave surround to fireplaces and doorways. Although not in themselves closely dateable, these elements mark a clear departure from the style and details of the 1630s work.

Building the Riding House Range

It is likely that the Riding House Range formed part of this post-war reconstruction in the early 1660s, perhaps even conceived before William's return in 1660 (its roof timber was felled some time between 1653 and 1678). Richard Bassano, writing in the 1680s, was in no doubt that 'Amongst other ye Stately buildings those raised by the thrice Noble & Puisant Prince Will[ia]m Duke of New Castle after his returne out of Exile The Stables, Riding House and Smithery w[i]th ought to be notice taken off.' The architectural motifs introduced into the reworking of the Terrace Range hall also appear in the Riding House Range. There are also innovations, particularly the style of window surrounds, which was new to Bolsover. A few undated documents in the Cavendish archives refer to the construction of the riding house, while others refer to a 'New Buylding' in distinction to a 'New ould building' (the Terrace Range) and an 'ould Building' (the Little Castle). The estate map of 1630–37 shows, schematically, a range in this location, but this was probably a comparatively insubstantial service range – most likely stables, a bakehouse and a brewhouse to support the 1630s buildings.

Rebuilding the State Apartment

The state apartment, as seen today, represents the final step in William Cavendish's developing taste, inspired by Italian Mannerist architecture. When William was living in Rubens's house in Antwerp, he probably acquired the artist's book *Palazzi di Genova*, first published in 1622, and – significantly – reprinted in Antwerp in 1652, which contained engravings of the palaces in Genoa.

We know from documentary evidence that Samuel Marsh was the architect, doubtless collaborating, as did his predecessors, with William himself. The state apartment is built up against the west end of the Riding House Range, whose intended eastern end was never finished. The eastern gable wall was left ragged for its continuation beyond a passageway, but not even its foundations were laid. Instead the present gateway was inserted in the gap, its style linking it to the new state apartment backing onto the re-roofed gallery.

William's honours and lands were returned to him by Act of Parliament on his return from exile in 1660. Building was in hand between 1663 and 1666, and the arms over the great court doorcase express William's elevation to the rank of Duke of Newcastle upon Tyne in March 1665. The reason for the sudden change of plan and style remains a mystery, for William must have known about Rubens's book while living in his house in Antwerp. Perhaps, as he came to know the new architectural landscape of England, and appreciate his continental experience, he decided a greater break with the past was needed, or that such full-blown Italian Mannerism was more suited to a state apartment.

Rebuilding Nottingham Castle

William had bought Nottingham Castle 'quite ruined and demolished' in 1663, but perhaps because of a lack of funds, he did not begin work on a new building there until 1674. Designed in collaboration with Marsh in the same Italian Mannerist style as his latest work at Bolsover, it was also perched high, on the castle rock, with its principal floor substantially occupied by a state apartment. In many ways it was the final distillation of ideas worked out at Bolsover – a building conceived for the royal entertainment of an earlier age when, unlike Charles II, the monarch made progresses through the kingdom.

Henry Duke of Newcastle

BOLSOVER UNDER THE 2ND DUKE OF NEWCASTLE

William Cavendish died in 1676 and Bolsover passed to his son Henry, who used it occasionally. Henry was an active Tory politician, loyal to Charles II and James II, but refusing the oath of allegiance to William and Mary. He was a man of 'unsteady fickle humour' who fell out with both his father and his wife. By 1683 he had completed Nottingham Castle in accordance with William's will, and wrote from Bolsover on 9 September 1687 that he had time on his hands 'to goe to my new stable and I saw the place for hay and conveniences in that poor old building, which Cornelius Farr [his steward] has contrived very well'. This seems to refer to the conversion of the stable to apartments, which led to changing most of the gallery to a stable, part of the former state apartment to a hay store, and the north end of the gallery and the kitchen below to a brewhouse. These events suggest that after Henry had completed Nottingham Castle he considered the state apartment at Bolsover redundant. Its contents had certainly been removed by 1717, when a full inventory of Bolsover was made.

BOLSOVER IN DECLINE

Duke Henry died in 1691, heavily in debt. He left his entire estate to his favourite daughter, Margaret, wife of John Holles, 4th Earl of Clare,

made 1st Duke of Newcastle upon Tyne of the second creation in 1694. John died in 1711 and on the death of his widow in 1716, Bolsover passed to their daughter, Henrietta. By this time the furnishings of the Little Castle were described as 'old', while those of the Terrace Range lodgings were variously referred to as very old, moth-eaten or rotten. Henrietta married Edward, Lord Harley, who became 2nd Earl of Oxford in 1724. She repaired the buildings, completely renewing the roof of the Little Castle between 1750 and 1751. Its architecture inspired some of her work at Welbeck, from which it remained a place of resort. She bought some new furniture for the Little Castle: at her death in 1755 the Marble Closet had a 'Tea Acquipage with a Dutch tea kettle and lamp'.

When Henrietta died in 1755, Bolsover passed once again through the female line to her daughter, Margaret, wife of the 2nd Duke of Portland; it stayed in the ownership of successive Dukes of Portland until the mid 20th century. The Little Castle remained habitable but the Terrace Range was unroofed by 1770. At this point, the stable seems to have reverted to its original location in the Riding House Range and the riding

Left: Henry, 2nd Duke of Newcastle, son of William Cavendish, who inherited Bolsover in 1676, shown here in a 17th-century portrait, attributed to Mary Beale
Below: *Portrait of Henrietta, Countess of Oxford, in riding habit. She inherited Bolsover in 1716 and repaired the roof of the Little Castle*

'[We found] the most dismal desolation, wainscots torn down, windows rattling in every pane, doors off their hinges', and began to 'convert the old, windy, rambling, desolate looking Norman castle into a habitation fit for civilised man'.
John Hamilton Gray, writing about his arrival at Bolsover

house itself was used as a hay barn. The 3rd Duke of Portland used Bolsover as a stud farm. Around this time the crenellated parapets on the terrace and garden walls began to be lost.

Internal walls began to be removed from the Terrace Range in the 1770s, but before much damage was done the 3rd Duke decided to keep it as a roofless ruin. It began to appear in guidebooks to Derbyshire and the Peak and was saved by the growing interest of antiquaries and tourists in pursuit of picturesque and romantic places.

THE LITTLE CASTLE AS A VICARAGE
The Duke of Portland paid the vicar of Bolsover's stipend; and since the parsonage was a 'small, mean house', by 1818 the vicar, William Calcroft Tinsley, had persuaded the then duke to let him become tenant of the Little Castle. Tinsley became 'miserably addicted to intemperate habits' (alcohol), and in 1829 his curate, John Hamilton Gray, paid him £25 to leave the castle for the parsonage. Gray succeeded as vicar in 1833.

The Grays found the Little Castle in a very poor state of repair. They added an entrance porch on the south front, which became the principal approach, through the garden. Most alterations to the connections between rooms in the Little Castle and the installation of sash

windows probably date from this period, particularly in the forecourt lodges, which served as domestic offices. Nearly all these works were subsequently obliterated by the Ministry of Works after 1945, apart from some sash windows on the north front, including those in the Pillar Parlour,

behind Gothick screens. The Grays seem to have been responsible for the garden layout as it was recorded in 1903 by the architect FW Gregory, with kitchen gardens in the Fountain Garden and part of the great court, the remainder of which was grassed over with trees and shrubs round the paths.

Despite these alterations, the Grays proved effective guardians of the place. The buildings appeared in romantic books, such as Nash's *Mansions of England in Olden Time*, and in architectural publications, contributing to the Jacobean revival. After Gray's widow left in 1882, the castle was entrusted to a caretaker living in the east end of the Riding House Range. The riding house roof was repaired, giving rise to the present open roof, and served as a temporary church between 1896 and 1897, while St Mary's Church was rebuilt following a fire. The western (stable) section of the Riding House Range had lost most of its roof by 1827, the shell later housing a forge and pig sties.

BOLSOVER FROM THE 20TH CENTURY TO THE PRESENT DAY

Bolsover was little more than a large village until the opening of Bolsover Colliery in 1889 and the

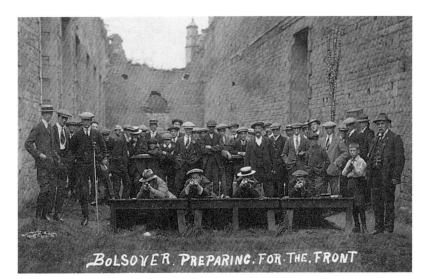

BOLSOVER. PREPARING. FOR. THE. FRONT

building of the garden village in 1893. Its population peaked in the early 20th century and, increasingly, the castle provided recreation for this industrial community. By 1903 the riding house was 'used as a drill room, and has been fitted up by the present Duke of Portland as a gymnasium for the Boys' Brigade. It is also used occasionally for amateur theatricals, and has a stage erected at its north-east end.' During the First World War the gallery was used as a rifle range and by 1918 the castle yard housed a bowling green and a tennis court.

Above: Local men from Bolsover village in the gallery, which was used for rifle practice during the First World War

Below left: The castle as the backdrop to the Coalite plant, photographed in 1992

The castle and town are built on a seam of limestone, overlying a layer of clay, which is visible at the foot of the scarp. The effects of mining exacerbated the tendency of the plate of rock to fracture into blocks, which move apart or slip from the edge of the scarp. By the 1920s massive cracks began to threaten the stability of the castle buildings. In 1936 the Coalite plant was established nearby to produce smokeless fuel, which damaged the castle stonework with acidic pollution.

By the time the 6th Duke of Portland died in 1943, the castle's future seemed precarious. Disaster was averted by its gift in 1945 to the Ministry of Works, and, over the next 40 years, the ministry and its successors stabilized the structures and gradually opened the site to the public. Under the direction of Patrick Faulkner, the Little Castle was tied together with 65 steel rods passing from side to side, and the cracks were grouted. It is a tribute to all involved that these repairs are invisible, but it is unfortunate that all the chimneys were stiffened by filling them with lightweight concrete, making it impossible to use any of the fireplaces. The riding house roof was repaired and reassembled bay by bay, the wall heads now tied together with a concrete ring beam. The Terrace Range was cleared of rubble and stabilized, and the parapets were replaced on the terrace wall.

The Miners' Strike of 1984 brought the coal industry to an unexpectedly rapid end, with Bolsover Colliery, the last in the area, closing in 1993. The Coalite plant lingered on until 2004. The era of industrialization had lasted only a century, and the threat it posed to Bolsover Castle's survival was gone, but at great social and economic cost to the local community.

With the major repairs completed, English Heritage has invested in improving the presentation of the site. The parapets on the wall-walk have been restored, offering views out over the landscape; the Little Castle garden has been replanted with period plants; the Star Chamber has been refurnished; and horses have once again become a regular sight at Bolsover.